DEDICATION

To Emily, thank you for being the wind beneath my wings.

TABLE OF CONTENTS

Chapter 1- Identifying Difficult People Everywhere

They are out there. They may either be your boss, college professor, business partner, landlord, or even your own spouse, children, siblings or parents. Anyone can be a difficult person to someone else. You may not admit it - but at one time or another; all of us have been difficult people to other people. Who knows, you may be seeking a remedy for difficult individuals you know without being aware that you're a difficult person yourself. It is vital to see if you are in a situation with a difficult person or if you yourself are beginning to be one.

The first solution to any problem is recognizing the problem. There was a man deep in a forest, who, one very dark, moonless night, lost his footing, stumbled and fell. When he hit the ground he found himself on an incline and began to roll. As he rolled downhill, over stones and bush, he was all the time picking up speed. At the last moment the earth disappeared below him and his roll turned into a fall. He started grasping for anything he could grab. Suddenly he bounced off of some kind of tree or shrub and he grabbed wildly, snagged a tree limb, and hung on for dear life. His fall was stopped, but he felt himself hanging in a dark void, feeling certain that if he let go he would certainly die as he crashed onto a rocky bottom he imagined thousands of feet below.

When the sun came up, he found the ground below him was a mere foot away from his feet. Had he known his real situation, he wouldn't have had to dangle there all night. Most difficult people do not realize they are difficult. They don't see that they are demanding too much from other people. They think their attitude is just normal. Likewise, some of their victims may not see that they are dealing with difficult people.

The earlier the problem is detected, the smoother the sailing will be. Smooth sailing, but you're still at sea. It's vital that at this early point, we grasp the fact that avoiding difficult people does not solve the problem in question. As earlier mentioned, these people are everywhere. There is no privacy they cannot invade. You might as well leave the planet and settle on Mars to get rid of them totally. But that will only mean you're going to start a new race of difficult people there. If you like the sea, you have to get used to its moods. The key is not to stay out of it but to learn to sail smoothly through thick and thin.

Likewise, it is learning how to deal with a difficult person that gives you smooth sailing amid a storm. Once you master this, difficult people will start liking you, and your new problem will be "how not to be liked too much" by difficult people. There is great reward in taming a difficult person. Remember The Little Prince?

The Types of Difficult People You Need To Be Aware Of and How to Deal with Each

Braggarts and blowhards, whiners and naysayers -- they're hard to work with and hard to live with. Here are ten of the most common types. One thing to remember when you read through these types is that these are behavior patterns people resort to when they're feeling threatened or frustrated. All of us resort to these once in a while.

The Big Bully

These people can ruin any day and any project. Whether they've contributed anything themselves or not, they come on full blast with criticism and accusations. They have only negative things to say about you and what you've done, and they think they've come to save the day. As people stand paralyzed around them, they take over and start to bark orders. Soon, however, they lose interest and move off in another direction. With everyone demoralized around you, you are left to pick up the pieces.

Dealing with the Big Bully:

The big bully is usually the type of person who is driven to get things done. When he feels thwarted in accomplishing something, he strikes out in general. Very often it's not personal at all, it's just his way to get something done. If you are under attack by the big bully it is because he sees you as part of the problem. Whether the bully is your boss at work or your spouse, he sees nothing wrong with his actions. He's forging ahead to complete a task.

To the big bully, the end justifies the means. When you are in the bully's line of fire, you might be tempted to counterattack. This is not the best idea since you might only incite him further. Justifying your position at this moment won't work well either because the bully doesn't want to hear your explanations. He wants results, and you sound like you're giving him excuses. That could infuriate him even more. When faced with an overbearing bully, many people shut down, say nothing, and slink off.

This is a very bad reaction to the bully because it solves nothing. This reaction makes the bully believe that he is justified. Your best approach in this situation is to hold your ground because bullies will not attack people they respect. You want to be assertive without becoming a bully yourself. This will impress the big bully and he will respect you now and in the future. Second, the next thing to do is to repeat the bully's name to him. Say his name firmly and clearly until he stops attacking - now you have his attention. Third, learn the bully's main concern. Quickly and clearly make it known that you understand what his complaint is. Then answer the complaint with a clear brief explanation. Finally, let him know that you're open to further discussion when he can speak to you with respect.

The Ambush Artist

If you've spent any time in business, you probably know this type. You've worked hard and long on a project for weeks and are unveiling it to the group. Out of nowhere the Ambush Artist shows up and begins to tear your presentation apart. This person specializes in saying just the right thing to destroy your credibility with a comment or a snicker. She seems innocuous, but she's double-barreled trouble.

Dealing with the Ambush Artist:

This difficult person is a backstabber when he feels threatened or left out. This person often attacks out of envy. Since it's not a frontal attack, you might not even know it is happening. But if you do happen to walk into an ambush, here's the way to handle it.

First of all, not all ambushes are equal. Sometimes the ambush is just attention-getting or trying to make people laugh at somebody else's expense, and sometimes it is more serious. Either way, this sniping is easier for some people to take than others. But it would be a mistake to either strike back or run away. The best way to deal with the Ambush Artist is to learn to have no emotional reaction because if you don't react, it's no fun for the Artist. The best way to handle the situation is directly and assertively. If you hear a remark about you, stop what's going on, find the person who made the remark, address her directly, and say something like," I think I heard you say… What exactly did you mean by that?" Be matter-of-fact but firm. If you're in the middle of a presentation, go through the same process and say,"

How is that relevant to what we're talking about here?" Again, you're being matter-of-fact but firm. At this point, the Ambush Artist will either back off, keep sniping, or become aggressive. If she backs off, go on with what you were doing before the interruption. If she keeps sniping, keep confronting her directly and asking what the point of her remark is. After a few of these confrontations, she will very likely stop sniping. If she comes out more aggressively with some comments, at least you brought it out into the open. Handle this the way you would Big Bully. Hold your ground, reply to the accusation, and ask to meet about it at an appropriate time. Then go back to what you were doing.

The Volatile Volumizer

This person is disruptive and confusing because he takes an ordinary situation and blows it out of proportion with hostility that is inappropriate to what is actually going on. This is the person who throws a fit when they get his coffee order wrong at Starbucks for his lunch order wrong at McDonald's.

Dealing with the Volatile Volumizer:

The Volatile Volumizer is an exploder. Like the Big Bully, his eruption frightens the people on the receiving end of the explosion, and they either explode back or disappear. The Volumizer feels unappreciated and powerless. Some people explode infrequently; others do it on nearly a daily basis. Losing control like these results in self-loathing for the Volumizer, but, nevertheless, the cycle begins to build again.

Your best approach with the Volatile Volumizer is to get some emotional distance and take control of the situation. Be friendly and calm as you say his name to get his attention. As you repeat his name, he will start to calm down and begin telling you his immediate concerns. Address these concerns clearly and quickly. The Volumizer will probably calm down fairly quickly because he is as uncomfortable with his behavior as you are. As he begins to calm down, you can decrease your own intensity. Take a time out so he can calm the rest of the way, but tell the Volumizer that you will discuss his concerns in the near future.

Finally, during your later discussion, try to discover what sets the Volumizer off. If you can find the cause, you may be able to prevent future outbursts.

The Know-It-All-Non-Listener

This person knows the answer to a problem without ever hearing about the actual problem. He might ask for advice, but he won't listen when it's given. He won't be corrected, and when things go wrong, he knows who to blame - you.

Dealing with the Know-It-All-Non-Listener:

This difficult person is often an expert or very knowledgeable in her field, and assertive and outspoken. She has grown used to basking in her expertise and considers any question to be a challenge to her authority. She has next to no tolerance for new ideas she hasn't presented. Being wrong is a humiliation to her and she protects herself by avoiding questions.

With the Know-It-All Non-Listener you might be tempted to confront her by throwing her attitude back at her or you might be inclined to resent her for her arrogance. This type of difficult person requires you to be patient and flexible and to present your ideas in a way that won't threaten her. Realize that this closed-off person is doomed to fight a losing battle since there will always be new ideas to threaten her. Think about your previous experiences with this difficult type. What worked?

Your goal here is to open her mind with new ideas while remaining non-threatening to her. You must be very knowledgeable about the ideas you are presenting or she will not hesitate to shoot you down. Then, you need to present your ideas with the utmost respect since this person has a very fragile ego. Present your ideas clearly and quickly but deferentially. Soften your statements with words like "maybe" and "What do you think?" so that it doesn't sound like you are presenting your ideas as a challenge to her. Your approach certainly demands patience, but as you continue to use this method, it becomes easier. As time goes on and your ideas are accepted, you will gain respect in her eyes. If you manage to turn this Know-It-All Non-Listener into a mentor, it can be a win-win situation for both of you. You will have a better relationship with her, and she will benefit from your good ideas.

The Wishy Washy One

You've probably met this person at least once. This person can't be pinned down no matter how hard you try. She's hard to work with because she won't meet project deadlines; she's just as hard to have a bake sale with because she can't decide on her share of the goods.

Dealing with the Wishy-Washy:

Decisive people are realistic about making decisions and know that every decision has an up side and a down side. Indecisive people like Wishy-Washy are so afraid of a negative result that they can't bring themselves to make a decision. They procrastinate about making a decision until it's too late to make one, and the entire project suffers. If you are managing the project or a coworker with Wishy Washy on the project, anger and impatience on your part is only natural. But that approach won't get you far with Wishy Washy. He will only stall and come up with more doubts. You need to approach Wishy Washy with patience and a sincere desire to help. This will allow him to trust you so that he can relax and think clearly. At this point, he'll be much more able to make a decision. He'll be in a better mood to go the next mile -- to allow you to teach him a system for making decisions.

Provide a comfort zone for Wishy Washy where he feels your genuine concern. Patiently discuss with him his conflicts about making a decision. Try to understand the basis for his objections. Show him a few systems that will help him make decisions. It could be as simple as a list of pros on one side of a page and a list of cons on the other. Reassure him that the decision he is making is a good one and no decision is perfect.

Let Wishy Washy know that you'll be happy to have these discussions in the future while he is learning decision making. This difficult person can turn out to be an excellent decision maker with a little practice.

The Yes Me to Death Fraud

These people are infuriating because they seem to be the nicest people around. They'll offer to do anything for anyone. They want to keep everybody happy. They'll do anything to avoid confrontation. But when it comes to delivering on the things they said they would do, what they deliver is excuses. They over-commit themselves so they have no time to actually do what they promised. Then they're surprised when you resent them for it.

Dealing with the Yes-Me-To-Death Fraud:

Yes Me To Death Frauds usually are sincere when they agree to do something, but if you've ever been sabotaged by somebody who promised to do something and didn't deliver, you know how infuriating it can be. Yes people over commit because they're trying to fulfill the desires of others. They don't think beyond the present moment so they don't realize that they can't possibly fulfill everything they've committed themselves to do. They just can't say no.

Yes Me To Death people are nice people. They want everything to work out. When it doesn't, they make excuses and wonder why people are angry. It's natural to be angry about broken commitments, but blaming and shaming the Yes Me To Death Fraud will only bring forth more promises and more excuses. Your approach with this person has to be one of kindness. You must realize that this person does not really mean any harm but is a people pleaser with no organizational skills. You need to make the Yes Me To Death person feel safe so she can be honest with you while you discuss her problem together. Then give this person some training in how to be organized. It will take a little of your time to show her some specific action steps and processes, but with some training this person is capable of saying no to too many projects and managing her tasks.

A good way to ensure commitment from this person is to ask for her word of honor. That's a deep level of commitment and will be meaningful to her. You might want to ask her to write the commitment down and sign it. If there's a deadline involved, she should write that down too. If there are any negative consequences for not completing the project on time, you should make her aware of those. Build a relationship with this difficult person so that if and when she overextends herself, she can feel safe coming to you and discussing it. This person is a genuinely nice person who can be turned into a staunch ally with the little training.

The Think They Know But Don'ts

These people love to dominate meetings or parties. They believe they know what they're talking about, and they sound so sure of themselves that it takes someone with some real expertise to know that what they are saying is empty and wrong. Their goal is to get attention, and they fool enough people so that they usually succeed.

Dealing with Those Who Think-They-Know-But-Don't:

Above all, these people want to be appreciated. They want attention and are very assertive about getting it. This is the type of person who knows just enough to be dangerous. When you first listen, he sounds like he knows what he's talking about. He's pretty convincing too since he himself believes he knows what he's talking about. Sometimes listening to this type of difficult person can be funny, but if something needs to be done correctly and it's crunch time, this person loses his charm. Then it becomes a vicious circle. People don't have the time to listen to him, and the less they listen to him, the more he craves attention. It's natural to be infuriated by this difficult person with his exaggerations and lies, but that won't get you anywhere. If you confront him aggressively, he will only exaggerate more and become louder.

Your best approach is to catch him when he's giving out misinformation and, without putting him on the defensive, put a stop to it. Ask him questions that will clarify some specifics and show that he doesn't know what he's talking about. Be sure to ask in an innocent manner since if he feels humiliated, your approach will backfire. The next step is to correct what this difficult person said with the facts as you know them. At this point give him a way out by saying something like, "That's fairly new information and maybe you haven't read it yet." If there's something you can thank him for, you should do it. He will appreciate being appreciated. Then get back to a discussion of the facts.

This tactic can work out well for you because when this difficult person sees that you know what you're talking about, he may become a fan of yours. The final step with this difficult type is to quietly let him know that his behavior has negative consequences for the group. At the same time, continue to give him reinforcement with the good things he does. That's really what he is looking for.

The Deep, Deep Freeze

This person is the strong silent type in a bad way. It's impossible to get them to hold up their end of the conversation. They have no opinion, good or bad. They are like the little boy who didn't talk until age six and when asked why, he said, "Up till now I've had no complaints." These people are hard to work with and hard to live with.

Dealing with the Deep, Deep Freeze:

This difficult person can be infuriating as she silently stares past you as if you were not there. This Deep Deep Freeze is a passive person, afraid of rocking the boat. She can also be a perfectionist who thinks that nothing measures up and withdraws in frustration. She seems to withdraw from confrontation but could be full of hostility inside.

Children are good at practicing this behavior. When a parent is intense about trying to correct a child, the child often withdraws into complete silence. The parent's behavior escalates in frustration, and the child goes further away and may even become completely unaware of what the parent is saying. This difficult type exhibits similar behavior.

Your goal is to get this person to talk. This will not be quick and easy, so if you need information from her, get it when you have some extra time. The first step you should take is to ask open-ended questions because these are more likely to elicit an answer. Ask questions that start with who, what, where, when, and how, since these words and open up topics for discussion. As you ask questions, make sure that you look and sound like you expect an answer. If everything else fails, you can try some humor. You could make some exaggerated guesses about why this person is the silent. That might break the ice. You could also make some guesses about what the person is thinking – all in a humorous way so that the person might break her silence. Whether you try this tactic depends on your own intuition about the situation.

Finally, you should gently try to show the Deep Deep Freeze that there are consequences to her silence. Show him what his silence is costing in terms of time wasted and lack of input from him. When the Deep Deep Freeze finally begins to talk, you should listen. You might get a lot of insight into why he's silent. This information could fend off these situations in the future.

The No, Not, Never Person

These people approach life with such futility and hopelessness that they give up before they even try. They are the ones who shoot down every good idea, whether it's at a meeting or presentation. They are so sincere in their belief that things won't work; they can't understand why you don't see it, too.

Dealing with the No,-Not-Never-Person:

The No, Not, Never person is usually a perfectionist who wants to get things right and not make mistakes. This person has high standards for what should be done, when it should be done, who should do it, and how it should be done which are not measured up to in life. So this difficult person believes everything will go wrong now and in the future.

This difficult person has a wide-ranging effect because negativity affects everybody around him. He is not intentionally trying to ruin things for everyone; he genuinely believes that things are as hopeless as he thinks they are. Your goal in working with this difficult person is to move him from fault finding and negativity to problem solving and improvement. It's probably very tempting to come out and tell Mr. No Not Never that things aren't nearly as bad as he thinks they are. But that would be a bad idea. Studies have shown over and over that when you try to make this person more positive, you only end up becoming more negative yourself. He will drag you down.

One way to look at this person is to see him as an early warning signal of trouble. Many times the No Not Never person sees flaws that really there. As for dealing with his negativity, you can try one of two tactics: bring up the negatives before he does or agree with him about the hopelessness of the situation. Tell him that he couldn't possibly sell this product – he might surprise you, and give it a try. Appreciate this difficult person for his good intentions and for having such high standards and for his willingness to speak up about details he's concerned with.

The Complaint Central Person

We all know at least one of these. These people complain about everything. Life is very hard for them, and they feel overwhelmed. This is because they are perfectionists and reality never measures up to what they have in mind. They complain to you and everyone else, but what they want is not so much solutions as to vent.

Dealing with the Complaint Central Person

The complaint central person is a lot like the No Not Never person because they both want to get things right. But Complaint Central has no idea about what to do to make things right. This gives him a feeling of helplessness which inspires his customarily whiny voice. If you have complainers in your life, you know how frustrating it can be. You can't agree with them because it makes them complain all the more. You can disagree with them, but they will only repeat what they said before. You can't solve their problems for them because they won't let you. Although it may be difficult for you, the best approach is to have patience, compassion, and commitment to the process of getting them to look for solutions.

First, you should listen to the complainer's main points. This shows them that you are interested. The next step is to get specific about the complaints. Let the complainer know for sure that he has been heard. Then shift the focus to finding solutions. This is the time to ask very specifically what he wants. If the solutions are completely unrealistic, show that to him and ask again what he wants. Do this until he comes up with a reasonable answer and then ask him what he's going to do to make that solution come true. If the complainer is incapable of coming up with solutions, put an end to the meeting at that time, saying, "You don't seem to have the solutions right now, but let me know when you come up with some." Complaint Central needs to understand that constant complaining is not acceptable and that solutions do exist.

CHAPTER 2- WHERE DOES THE DIFFICULTY COME FROM?

The first thing we need to do to improve relationships with difficult people is to understand where they're coming from. People behave based on what they're thinking. Their behavior can change very quickly as their thoughts change, but understanding their frame of mind is the place to start. Everyone has a wide range of behavior including normal behavior and behavior under difficult circumstances.

There are four types of intent being at the root of the behavior. The four types of intent include getting it done, getting it right, getting along, and getting appreciation. Depending on what they want at the time, difficult people can shift from one of these states to another. You can easily tell where people are coming from by looking at their communication style.

- In the "get it done" mode people are focused on a task to be completed. Communication is brief and to the point.

- In the "get it right" mode focus is on the details of the task, with documentation to prove the task has been done correctly.

- In the "get along" mode the person is considerate of others' feelings and opinions.

- In the "get appreciated" mode the person has an elaborate style that calls attention to himself.

Clearly, if people who are working together have the same communication style, it would be smooth sailing. Problems arise when people with different communication styles or intent are working together. For instance, when people want to "get it done" and it's not getting done, they become more controlling. The Big Bully, The Ambush Artist, and The No It All Non-Listener all become more controlling when they feel threatened.

When people want to "get it right" and are afraid it's being done wrong, they become more perfectionistic. The Deep Deep Freeze, The No, Not, Never Person, and The Complaint Central Person all become more perfectionistic when they feel something is being done incorrectly.

When people want to "get along" and think they're being left out, they become more approval seeking. The Wishy Washy One and the Yes Me to Death Fraud become even more approval seeking when they feel they are being ignored or rejected.

What Makes Difficult People Difficult?
When people want "to be appreciated" and think they're not, they become more attention seeking. The Volatile Volumizer and the Think They Know It Alls try harder to get attention when they feel they are not being appreciated.

Have you noticed that while you're reading through this list of the 10 most difficult behaviors, you might have run into yourself? If we're going to be honest, don't we all whine, complain, procrastinate about making a decision, and all the other behaviors from time to time? The difference is probably that we don't do it as often as difficult people and we don't do it with the intensity they do. When we see ourselves acting this way, we often deliberately change our behavior. Difficult people become more difficult when they feel threatened and not understood, so how we interact with them is the key to them behaving at their best, not their worst. In the next chapter will take a look at how we can communicate with difficult people to bring out the best in them.

Chapter 3- Added Pressure, Added Level of Difficulty

When pressures in life start to get out of control, a difficult person is born. Babies are cute even when they start to mess around with things. But when they grow up, it's a totally different story. The same thing holds true for difficult people. They start out amusing, even witty, but most of them turn into monsters later— some overnight.

Life pressures are common. We all encounter them in certain measures, and the degrees vary each day. They help us mature gracefully, if handled well. But the moment it controls us, we tend to pass the pressure on to others and we become a pain in the neck, so to say.

The day you were born, the womb was pressured to the maximum and your mother had to be rushed to the delivery room. When you were transferred from the womb into this world, you were grown through a series of pressures: the pressure to eat, to sleep, to stop crying, to lie on your belly, to sit, to crawl, and to stand up and finally, to walk. Your parents had to force you to do these things as a part of growing up.

Then there's the pressure to eat nutritious things like vegetables and fruits. As you continued to grow, you were pressured to talk and pronounce words properly. Then, you were sent to school. There, the teacher introduced new pressures to you to help you learn more and be updated. The higher the schooling, the stronger the pressures became. Exams, projects, recitations, competitions, and the like were introduced to you, because more of those pressures will meet you in the future, they said.

You were born and grown through pressures. These pressures are all necessary. They are all good. They are designed to bring out the best in us. But somehow, when taken out of context or in the wrong perspective, they become negative pressures that, instead of bringing out the best, bring out the worse. Pressures ought to be faced maturely. This means the soul (mind, feelings, and will) is nurtured as pressures are overcome. But when the ego takes in all the beatings (the soul succumbs to the pressures), a difficult person emerges and takes over.

Naming and Charting Pressure

More often than not, life pressure is the culprit in the emergence of difficult people.

Other types are:

•Peer pressure when being difficult becomes a trend (glorified in movies and on TV) and your peers go with the flow.

•Illness pressure Which is due to a mild illness.

•Disciplinary pressure

Having a difficult attitude is assumed to test the loyalty and perseverance of subordinates, such as in offices, in fraternities, or in the military. These pressures are often momentary and feigned. Disciplinary pressures seldom result to a bad attitude because it is used to mold the character.

•Overt Pressures

Some pressures in life are obvious. They attack from the outside. Piled up work in the office, a very demanding boss, deadlines to beat, school or board exams, and a nagging wife are examples of these pressures. They are often temporary and manageable, cut by rest periods when the cause of the pressure is allayed. But they show nonetheless, sometimes in slightly heightened degrees. And yes, some difficult people may also be a result of other people's being difficult to them. It's like a vicious cycle – in most cases it is attributable to attitude transfer. Wrong attitudes can be imparted.

Overt pressures are mostly "skin deep" and can rarely affect the total person for long periods. More so, it is seldom permanent. Bad attitude from this pressure feeds on the periodic onslaughts of minute pressures, and without such feeding the bad attitude subsides. But if ignored, such bad attitude may worsen as the ratio of pressures and rest periods become disproportional. In such case, the bad attitude recovers quickly from the rest period because the latter is cut short by a new overt pressure. For instance, a student is pressured by both financial problems and the submission of a school project due soon. He is irked by financial woes and lack of time.

Such double or even multiple pressures produce low LOT. He starts to be prickly with his group mates. After rushing to finish the

What Makes Difficult People Difficult?

project the night before the deadline, the professor announces a long surprise quiz. The first pressures have hardly gone by when the second one comes in. The rest period is terribly cut short, leaving the battered emotions unrelieved, and the temperament all the more irritated. The LOT drops to its lowest point. When a person is pestered by overt pressure and he has the will to initially overcome it, he tends to be mildly difficult at first. LOT slightly lowers. If symptoms persist and complications are added, he goes halfway to being extreme. It becomes extremely difficult to stop when the pressures start to really build up. The LOT dives as a result.

When the pressure increases, the LOT decreases; and vice-versa. If a person has control of his LOT and is able to even boost it, he has mastered the art of self-control and proves to be a strong, patient person we all admire. Most pressures are uncontrollable, but our levels of toleration are - if we master them. And once we do, we are able to help difficult people. So the game is really all about LOT mastery. And winning the game means keeping the LOT high up. A high LOT is a sure way of determining that you are not a difficult person, and a high LOT is a sure tactic for conquering difficult people.

For instance, if any one of these occurs:

•A demanding boss or professor (probably a difficult guy himself) is appeased,

•A deadline is met

•An exam is passed and then things quiet down, and the difficult person relaxes and exhibits tolerable manners.

Often, these ease periods that occur between pressures are relief well taken by him so that he may sometimes be strangely benevolent to people. You may see him being nice even to people he despises. He may display acts of kindness or generosity, such as buying everyone lunch. But don't be deceived. Such transitions are temporary. Brace up for another round of challenges soon. Overt pressures are at times easy to escape from.

Difficult people who meet such pressures usually resort to other activities to divert attention and be temporarily relieved from the pressures that beset them. They may busy themselves with some charitable works, games, leisure or hobby. They may take up a new school course, or socialize and hold positions in clubs. Initially, this seems a good way of "channeling energy" to other "positive" activities, but this is a mere escape route that can change or solve nothing except give short relief.

There are crucial factors affecting overt pressures. Among them are:

- Escapism.

As Karl Marx puts it, anything that diverts attention from the root cause of a problem is an "opiate." Escapism is not only an opiate, it drowns its victims in a whirlpool of falsehood and lies which later transform the person and become real in a victim's eyes. Many difficult people worsen when they resort to mere escapism to ward off pressures without confronting and remedying their situation. The brief relief diminishes in effectiveness. Higher doses of relief are required to produce a more potent anti-pressure in the same way that antibiotics become ineffective when overused. Thus, you often see difficult people becoming harder to please. When difficult people resort to escape, they are building their own world of lies. Worse, they impose these on other people, so that meaningful relations are only possible when others adapt to the world of these difficult people.

- **Crossing Over.**

Some overt pressures, if taken positively, can actually serve as "stepping stones" to help difficult people overcome their adverse attitudes. These are called stepping stones because they can slowly change a difficult person from being difficult to being tolerable or considerate. It's like crossing over from their false world to the real world.

- **Pressure Reversal**

When you fight negative tendencies, you reverse the pressure effects and, if done consistently, come out a different person. This takes a lot of self-control. Child psychologists say that instead of making a child obey you, you talk to them in suggestions that make sense based on their interests. For instance, you can make a child stop running by picking them up and sitting them in a chair. Or you can explain to them that running might cause them to stumble and hurt themselves – perhaps them telling them a story about someone injured by running in an inappropriate place. The child is now focused on ways to avoid getting hurt.

In pressure reversal, a person convinces themselves to always react positively especially in adverse situations. When you do this yourself, the goal is to not become like the difficult person you are dealing with. You don't want to turn into an unreasonably demanding boss someday, so you assume exactly the opposite attitude your difficult boss shows you. It takes an apple tree to produce an apple. If you want a banana, you won't find it on your apple tree. Likewise, you have to plant within yourself the type of person you want to become and nurture then nurture the seed.

How? Reason with yourself.

For instance, if you are a student facing your final exams, ask yourself: Do you want to pass your exams and get a degree just to become a rotten character? Do you want to become a difficult person or a difficult employer yourself? As you realize the pressure of studying for your exams, or during exam day itself, and find yourself becoming out of sorts, or testy, persuade yourself not to give in. Fight it off and bear in mind your goal of becoming agreeably different.

- Covert Pressures

These are pressures that are imbedded attack from within. They are the more subtle pressures that make for a more difficult and often defiant or resistant character. Difficult people born out of covert pressures seem to disagree with everybody and everything. They seem to hate the world. They seldom find respite from their pressures because the pressures are deep within. It has been built into their system. Unlike difficult people with overt pressures who still enjoy intermediate (though temporary) cessation of pressures, victims of covert pressures live a life of being difficult. They stay hurt and irritated, and are quick to react negatively in many situations.

Covert pressures are often things in the past that were impressed during childhood, like abusive or damaging words from parents, scenes of violence, fierce sibling rivalry, discrimination, and persistent financial problems. Some may be incurred in adolescence or even in adulthood.

Covert pressures either push people to compete for recognition or to withdraw by blaming others. These people try to live a dream wherein everything is perfect due to their designs and doings. They see themselves as heroes who always know the right things to do. They dictate their ways and opinions on others while fully convinced they are here on a mission to correct others. People react to covert pressures in 2 ways. They either:

Compete for recognition.

Covert pressures may goad people to compete for recognition. Aching to be recognized is one highly motivational pressure that has either made or broken lives in history. A classic example is a boy who, due to poverty, suffered discrimination and banishment. His relatives made him feel that he would never amount to anything. As he grew up, the boy vowed to do everything to prove his accusers wrong. He later became a self-made man. Over the years he became successful materially but his hurt emotions had been imbedded within his ego. Now, life to him is one big competition. He constantly strives to show himself as right and others as wrong. Of course, he does not announce this as a creed, but without being aware it becomes the foundation of all he does. It becomes the engine that runs his life, the inspiration that gives him gusto. So he goes about his daily routine correcting everybody, giving his unsolicited advice, and making sure everyone listens to him. After all, he is a self-made man, and people ought to learn from his example. And thus the difficult life begins for those close to him and around him. Of course, any man under covert pressure can opt to react differently and apply a little pressure reversal. He may still do everything to win in life, but he must also consider those who are not as successful, and those who do not want to be too successful.

Withdraw by blaming others.

Covert pressures can also send people to the depths of despair; and being in a helpless state, they hate others for it. They may opt to appear defeated and view themselves as a loser. They may try to prove this to others by refusing to engage in anything worthwhile. Yet they maintain that they are mere victims of circumstances beyond control, of which others are to blame. It is often a life of endless searching for reasons to despair more. These difficult people see nothing but failure and doom, and urge you to see things likewise. Yet, they may also opt to appear normal like everybody and pretend to undertake worthwhile things. But they lead a life of constantly blaming others for everything wrong and claiming authorship for everything right. Often, these people will offer little help or suggestion, if any, unlike those who opt for competition for recognition. These individuals will only blame and put down people. They love to see failure mushrooming around people. They damage the emotional foundations of people. When ignored, they go deeper and settle in the egos. The ego, or inner person, is the one within that controls and operates the person outside. The visible person outside is a mere puppet of the person inside.

When the Overt and the Covert Meet

The worst scenario comes when both overt and covert pressures attack difficult people. Imagine a guy with a serious, covert pressure imbedded in his heart which grows as the years pass by. Then add the outside pressures that worsen the pressure inside. Hot steams begin to spill out of breaks in the walls. When the whole thing finally gives way, you have a volcanic eruption in your hands. In real life, there are such people. Pressures do wonders to people. Geological pressures beneath the earth either create violent upheavals. It is the same with pressures on humans. Pressures can transform people to better and stronger individuals, or they can stir them to chaotic impulses that create deadlier pressures. People who are able to break through barriers of pressures unharmed come out like diamonds.

CHAPTER 4- THE DIFFICULTY DISEASE – ACQUIRING THE VIRAL ATTITUDE

To further understand the mechanics of being a difficult person, it is necessary to know that some attitudes may be transferred, and any such transfer may result in a worse or better attitude. It is a law of nature.

Good cells always produce better, healthier cells. Bad cells produce worse cells, and worse cells produce dead cells later. A good tree produces good fruits, and a bad tree produces bad crops. Now, by putting the pressure reversal to work, the vicious cycle can be interrupted and can produce the exact opposite: • A good attitude can spring up from a bad attitude if the bearer simply decides to be different and works it out. • A bad tree may be treated with reversal treatments like grafting and spraying to make it bear good fruits. A difficult person is difficult probably because he got it from someone close to him:

- A difficult father may inadvertently transfer his personality to a child who either idolizes or abhors him. •

- A professor may transfer his attitude to his students. •

- You may acquire the characteristics of your friends.

Acquiring Difficulty from Your Hero

When a successful person is a difficult person, those who idolize him and follow in his footsteps may also turn out to be difficult individuals too. They will see that a factor in his success is his dealing with people. People always attribute their success partly to management skill. To others, management skills equate to how you talk to and treat people; or worse, putting pressure on people for them to work harder.

Likewise, a person who ends up in tragedy may appear successful to others as a hero because he personifies a cause they are fighting for. For example, a janitor, while trying to save his boss, dies in a fire. He may be idolized by his sons who would also become janitors loyal to their bosses. It is good to emulate really good heroes, but even difficult people can appear heroes to some people, and thus people imitate their attitude. Dictators have always left behind followers that may become even more ruthless.

Passing on the "I Hate" Attitude

World history is replete with people who deposed dictators only to become worse dictators themselves. There are two reasons for the transfer of this attitude:

1. Revenge. Some people who suffered at the hands of difficult people tend to repeat everything to their subordinates or to the next generation. Here works the Principle of Substitution. Imagine a rebel group overthrowing an oppressive government, with a new leader installed as the head of state. The quest for revenge would logically be taken out on those deposed. But imagine that they are now dead, or have fled the country and are no longer reachable, perhaps being protected by another government. The new leader may then take out his revenge on those under him who are powerless. Those under him become substitutes for the real object of vengeance. Hence, the child who suffers from his difficult father might release his frustration on his younger brother. The younger brother might take on his pet dog.

2. Holding on to power. Imagine a sales manager who hates his difficult boss, who has the title of sales director. The difficulty stems, in part, from the director taking credit for the sales of his subordinate, the sales manager. He does this in an effort to maintain his position of power. Then a change takes place and the sales manager is promoted to the position of sales director, replacing his former boss. He begins to love the position so much that he understands the attitude of his ex-boss and soon proves to be as difficult, or more difficult, than his predecessor. He is a victim of a difficult person and hates it. But he then becomes a more severe copy of the person who made life so difficult for him. Why? It is because he wants to hold onto power.

Chapter 5- Affecting Difficult People with Motivation

When we are speaking of motivation, we need to realize one very important thing. Motivating someone doesn't just help the motivated person to do better; it also helps other people who are associated with the person in some or the other way. For instance, if your spouse is motivated into starting a new business, and if that business starts bearing fruit, then the entire family is benefited. Here, just one person is motivated, but that motivation has helped a whole family. This can be extrapolated to larger scenarios.

A motivated leader of a company could benefit the entire organization. A motivated president could benefit the entire country. A motivated freedom fighter could bring about a revolution for the betterment of society and the world at large. Hence, motivating others is important to you. Especially if you are in some position of power and you deal with people all the time, then it becomes important for you to keep your people inspired. Only when they are inspired will they feel that they can do a good job for you and for the entire society or organization that you are a part of.

Motivating others is one of the chief challenges faced by leaders in the political and other arenas. Take the case of corporate leaders or chief executive officers. They are the people who head an organization and are in charge of its operations. They need to show results to their shareholders—results in terms of sales, profits and the social good achieved by their respective enterprises. But, the amount they can do by themselves is very limited. They therefore depend on their managers, subordinates and teams to get the job done and to meet the annual targets. Here is where the task of motivation comes in. Left to their own devices most workers will just shy off. It is something of a joke in Kolkata (India) that the babus or clerks take a 'break' from their continuous sessions of tea to do some work. So, one of the most vital tasks of the CEO is to motivate his team to deliver the desired results. If you want people to work and to work together as a team to achieve results in a specific time frame you need to use many ways to motivate them.

Successful motivation requires a combination of structure and incentives. It also calls for communication, communication, and communication. It is no longer just a carrot and stick approach. It requires special skills and cannot be done by any and every one. See if you can motivate your dog to fetch his bone for you and you will better appreciate how difficult it is to motivate humans.

Motivating others is a skill that is always rewarded with sweet success. Thus motivating others helps you achieve your own goals. It also gives you the satisfaction of having helped a fellow human being realize his own potential. Any CEO knows the value of this. People are the most valuable resource in any company. In addition, all people have some talent, which is usually hidden, lost under a pile of everyday routine. It is for the wise CEO to give all employees an environment in which their talents can bloom.

Moreover, when this happens, the employee become self-motivated and you cannot stop him from achieving his goals even if you tried to. In the terrorist attack on the Taj Mahal hotel Mumbai, in 2008, many employees laid down their lives in trying to help their clients out of the hotel safely. So remarkable is this that Harvard has actually commissioned a study to understand what motivated these employees to do so. A lot of the credit will go to the management obviously. The achievement of results, the satisfaction of a job well-done, the success of the enterprise, the altruistic rewards of helping your fellow men achieve self-actualization.

These are some of the benefits you will derive out of motivating others. It will help you head a team of people who are happy because they are involved in an enterprise and all rowing in the same direction. It will help you become a better person.

How to Motivate The Difficult to Be Better People

The most common visual you conjure up when you think of motivation is the carrot and the stick. This means using either rewards or punishment to get the job done or to make some behavioral change. But, today, as we learn more and more about people and human behavior we know that the task is far more complex than that. There are several things that you can do and others that are a complete no. Let us start with the latter. You should never threaten a person with dire consequences in order to get something done. Nothing is more guaranteed to get their backs up and to achieve the exact opposite results. Here are quite a few positive and useful tips on how to motivate people.

The Emotion Factor

Appeal to their love for acquiring things by providing concrete rewards - be they in the form of cash, kind or recognition. Let them know in advance if you are going to reward performance and make it amply clear what it is that is expected out of them. Then, when they deliver the results make sure you keep your word, reward them as per your promise.

Dole Out the Right Incentives

Performance incentives are a very powerful tool and if you treat your employees fairly they will go the extra mile for you. Make sure that your program is well structured, well communicated and well understood throughout the company. Make the goals achievable and divide into short term (low hanging grapes) and long term (annual harvest) goals. Discuss the goals and involve the employees in the goal setting exercise. That way you ensure buy in and the employees understand their stake in accomplishing the tasks that will help them reach the agreed goals.

Lend Them an Ear... Always

Always listen to your people and treat them with respect and kindness. Being arrogant and listening only to your own voice is as good as being blind and deaf. Be fair but firm. Deadlines need to be respected and a laissez-faire attitude will not do. Most importantly, reward them for working in teams. One plus one literally means three, maybe even four, in the context of the corporate world, as it is through interaction and sharing of knowledge that you arrive at the best and most innovative ideas and efforts. People also enjoy working with other people and when positive energy flows, it multiplies as the load is shared and work becomes fun.

Feed Them Back

Offer fair feedback without aiming to curtail their creativity. You need to be very sensitive when doing this or you could easily demotivate. Always, but always recognize achievement preferably in public. Give people space to produce results. Give them the tools and the resources and support them in their endeavors in every way you can. All these are factors that will motivate them to give you back in kind.

Best Communication at All Times

Ultimately, always keep the channels of communication open. This will enable you to learn of potential problems at an early stage and to fix them before the problem gets out of hand.

Chapter 6- Keeping the Communication Lines Open to Help Difficult People

There is less conflict and more cooperation between people who feel they are on the same page. There is a technique called blending where you mirror the other person's volume and speed when talking. We often do this automatically with people we like and trust. We can do this deliberately with difficult people to make them feel more comfortable. In the workplace there's very little blending with people who work together. People want to know that you are listening and understanding what they're saying.

A communication technique to let people know you are listening is to nod your head occasionally and make a sound like you understand, and then repeat back what they've said. Through this they know clearly that they've been heard.

What Makes Difficult People Difficult?

The next step is to repeat back some of the actual words that the other person is using. Using their actual words relate strongly to them that you have been listening.

The third step is to clarify what's been said. Now you can start asking questions to get further information. This will give you more specifics and asking the right questions can help the difficult person become more rational. Asking questions demonstrates that you are taking the other person seriously; asking the right questions can more quickly lead to a solution.

The fourth step is to summarize what you've heard. Repeating the discussion to the difficult person shows that you are both on the same page and gives the person a chance to fill in any blanks, any details that are missing. Since it shows once again that you are making a serious effort to understand, it increases the likelihood of the difficult person's cooperation.

The final step is to confirm the conversation by asking outright, "Do you feel understood?" This process is so deliberate and so focused on the difficult person and the issue, there's a great chance that you will receive cooperation from the other person.

Why Listening is a Powerful Tool in Dealing with Difficult People

Most of us would like to be thought of as clever or intelligent. Some people -- we all know one or two -- think that the way to make that happen is to be a smart aleck with lots of wise cracks. Actually, the opposite is true. The surest way to make the other person think that you are the most intelligent person he knows is to listen to him and pay attention to what he has to say. After all, if you're listening to him, you must be smart!

Listening gives the listener power in a few ways. This is even truer with difficult people. Most people, even difficult people, want you to know what their position is. We need to listen to learn his needs, but the problem is that difficult people set up uncomfortable situations with the result that we are even more likely to tune out. If you give people a chance, they will tell you what they want from you. In fact, since the days of Freud, psychologists have believed that if you can get the other person to talk enough, she will not be able to stop herself from telling you what's on her mind. The reverse is also true. If you don't want the other person to know what you're thinking, don't talk very much.

Listening can also help you overcome self-consciousness because if you're completely involved in what the other person is saying, the focus is off yourself. Here are some techniques that will make you a good listener in the eyes of the person talking:

1. Look at the person speaking. It helps you concentrate on what he's saying, and it becomes clear that you are listening with total attention.

2. Appear very interested in what is being said. Nod your head, smile when it's appropriate, and make a comment when asked.

3. Lean toward the person speaking. It's a natural tendency to lean toward an interesting speaker.

4. Ask questions. That's a clear indication to the speaker that you're listening.

5. Don't interrupt. Do the opposite -- ask him to tell you more. People are complimented when you draw them out.

6. Stick to the speaker's subject. This is another indication that you're interested.

7. Use the speaker's own words to get your point across. It shows you're listening, and it's a good way to get the speaker to agree with you.

Chapter 7- Harnessing the Will and the Power to Make a Difference

When we're talking about personal power here, we're not referring to force or intimidation. We're talking about the power we have to validate each other, and to satisfy each other's natural, universal ego hunger through acceptance, approval, and appreciation of each other. When we use this power successfully, it opens doors to everything we desire.

Most of us never understand that we have any power -- not over ourselves or over other people. A person who values other people will

What Makes Difficult People Difficult?

1. Acknowledge the value of others. Think of it this way: If you were the only person in the world, how much could you accomplish? How much more could you accomplish as one among billions? Does that drive the point home? Did you ever consider that power is about how others see you? If you want power, people must see you as powerful.

2. Make more of others -- this will make more of you. Give people credit when it's due. It doesn't take anything away from you. On the contrary, it shows that you are strong and generous. This makes people in general admire you, especially the ones you are giving credit to.

3. Accept people for who they are. That doesn't mean that you necessarily like them, but if you want others to give you the power you seek, you must give it to them as well by allowing them to be who they are without judging them.

4. Work on approval, even of people you don't like. Everyone has something about him or her that you can admire. When the other person feels your approval, he or she will give you the power you seek.

5. Appreciate others. Respect them and their time. See their individuality. When you give others the acceptance, approval, and appreciation you want yourself, you are improving your life. This is a self-fulfilling prophesy, and they will give acceptance, approval, and appreciation back to you. When you're dealing with difficult people, they will recognize your positive attitude toward them and reward you with their cooperation.

Why Running Away from Difficult People Won't Help

You must like people. Liking people is the first sure step to triumph. Avoiding people, especially the difficult ones, is a sure road to becoming difficult yourself. So go out and meet people. Greet them and genially accept whatever reaction they give you. Don't be discouraged but greet more of them regularly until you get used to them, and until your LOT skyrockets. Some people may prove to be difficult by being rude but this doesn't hurt you in any way. It only hurts them.

Smile.

Most touchy people can be neutralized by a friendly smile. So practice putting on a pleasant, simple, friendly smile in front of a mirror. Public speakers and actors study their facial expressions facing a mirror. Political and beauty aspirants take time with a photographer just putting on the best smile that exudes confidence and friendliness. A smile says it all. Regardless of how your face looks, a smile always puts on warmth and comeliness. A good smile always arrests the temper, even that of difficult people. So always smile.

Be sincere.

A smile helps a lot, but sincerity gives your smile credibility. A mere smile is a matter of facial muscle flexing. When this alone is involved, the smile becomes unnatural. Put your heart into it! A sincere heart will automatically show if you live a life of sincerity. Always be sincere in all you do daily. When your heart gets used to being sincere, smiling sincerely becomes natural. Difficult people can see right through you, and sincerity melts their hearts.

Listen well.

Almost every difficult people want to talk much more than they listen. This is the main problem in communication. Difficult people love to talk and want people to listen to them. In a nutshell that's what they are. Basically, you cannot put two difficult persons together and have them talk. Difficult people avoid each other once they recognize each other. If they are made to sit down and listen, they won't stand it. They will either stand up and steal the scene, or just walk out. If you are with a difficult person, then you should practice becoming a good listener. You must learn the wisdom of enjoying listening. Few have this wisdom. Most people think there is wisdom in monopolizing a conversation.

As in business, this only results in unfairness and silent protests. You can make difficult people happy when you just listen to them. Not many can do this. When you are a good listener, even the most difficult people tend to trust you with their secrets. Then you begin to know them as they reveal who they really are. You begin to understand them deeper and will be able to help them better.

Be agreeable.

This does not necessarily mean agreeing to anything difficult people say, but it is more about agreeing not to argue. If you don't agree with the opinions of difficult people, just listen and send everything to your mental bin. Delete. It's your right. Never argue. Never mind if they say you are not confrontational. So what? Nobody dies because of that. But arguments often kill. Nations go to war because of arguments. See the wisdom? Remember that every seed of kindness you plant now will surely reap a harvest of favors soon. Valuables are often left to agreeable people, never to aggressive ones. Very few trust contrary people. If you are known for your politeness, even the most difficult folks will give you special favors. Always remember that the most difficult people are strivers. They are workaholics. They feed on pressure to hit their goals. Oftentimes they get promoted to positions that confer favors on "worthy" men. They often rake in more valuables than the average guy.

Be honest.

Never flatter anyone insincerely, especially difficult people. Insincere flattery always traps its users, and it sure is hell to get trapped with a difficult person. Hence, it always pays to just listen and be agreeable. When difficult people ask your opinion or ask if you agree with them, tell them honestly but nicely. If you agree, agree. If you don't, make sure you stress that it is your opinion, not a statement of fact. Most likely, they will not agree with it and even make you realize how stupid it is. Just listen and be polite. Or, if possible and truthful, quote somebody's opinion that agrees with yours. If they mock it, at least you save your dignity. Then you can smile more easily. If you insincerely flatter difficult people and they get to like you for it, woe to you! You will find it more difficult, and later, impossible to be free from them.

Sing Praises Whenever Due

Be certain to take note of their worth and achievements, even if you think differently and have a different idea for success. Appreciate their efforts. Share their triumphs and sad moments. At times, a smile or tap of congratulations or sympathy is enough and speaks volumes. But never overdo it. Practice the steps above daily until you make it your habit. You will soon possess a healing power that countless people need and crave. The power that will launch you to untold successes in whatever endeavor you engage in.

Chapter 8- How to Avoid Becoming a Difficult Person Yourself

Respect people always.

Be aware that people, young and old, are entitled to their rights, beliefs, and opinions. Without being vocal about it, don't consider yourself to be better than others. This will get rid of self-conceit which is the root of disrespect and being inconsiderate. Respect authorities in their jurisdictions, whether in the office, school, malls, public buses, homes, or lands. Be aware that you cannot impose your own standards and you have to adjust to their policies.

Don't compare yourself with others aloud.

You may do so in your mind, but never actually say it. Different people mostly do things differently and you must not feel superior with your methods and style. Likewise, do not compare people with other people verbally. We have tendencies to compare people, but keep it to yourself.

Follow a schedule but don't be too rigid with it.

If you are an employer or supervisor, you will surely have work schedules and deadlines for your employees or subordinates. But don't be too harsh on the implementation. Remember that we are only humans – even machines and computers fail. People err, get tired or sick, and at times get burned out. They need encouragement. Give them workloads equal to what you pay them. Be kind to them. If you are in business, don't get too absorbed in hitting goals or quotas. There will always be tomorrow, and tomorrow will yield better results. Learn to let go of things that pressure you. Drop everything and go out for a while. Meditate. Look at your surroundings and enjoy them. Smile at people. There's more to life than just doing your business or anything else that keeps you stressed out.

Enjoy what you are doing, and make sure those working with you also feel the same way.

Work must support life, and not the other way around. When work becomes a burden, life merely supports work, and that will be painful for everyone. Then, sooner or later, everyone becomes a difficult person. Every job must become an adventure where every turn makes you excited to go further.

Never assume to know everything.

Even if you do, always consider what others have to say, even if you're a boss. Accept the fact that there are things you are utterly ignorant of, no matter how smart you think you are. If in a meeting among peers you are knowledgeable about a topic and they are not, it is safer to wait to be asked for your opinion. It is also good to politely offer your opinion, but do so more on a note of sharing rather than lecturing.

Never give unsolicited advice.

Don't give pieces of your "good" advice to people who don't ask for them, more so to people who don't look like they need them. Unless you are closely related to such people, or you are asked for your advice, keep your suggestions to yourself. You may need them more than anyone else does.

Learn to admit fault and apologize.

It's not important anymore to determine who is right and who is wrong. When you see that you have hurt a person, whether you are on the right or wrong side, admit your fault and apologize. Admitting your fault does not always mean you are wrong. It may mean you said the right thing at the wrong time in the wrong place. And that's your fault. It's definitely your fault when you come into a funeral wake and tell the bereaved that the dead man was a crook and a liar (difficult people can do this). You may be right, but your rightness will hurt the feelings of the aggrieved family, and that's your fault. It's different when the truth needs to be revealed in the name of justice. If you have to testify in court that the dead man was a crook and a liar, though it may hurt the relatives of the deceased, you must say so without hesitation.

Love must override rules and regulations.

True leaders love their followers and always seek after their welfare. They do not just put things in order. Many administrators and managers merely want order and to see to it that rules and policies are obeyed. This makes many of them difficult people. Rules and policies are good, but they seldom benefit anybody except maybe the ones who made them. Don't decide on matters in a way that negates the personal choices of other people, like in choosing a lifetime partner, a career, or things to buy. Guide them but never dictate them.

Don't be unreasonable.

Make sure your instructions and requirements are within reach and capacity of other people. You may be able to do certain things other people can't, and you have to consider this. Remember that you yourself also have limited potentials.

Never humiliate people.

Don't shout at people, or scold them, or curse them, especially in front of other people. It's normal to be angry at times when there is a valid reason. But be careful not to turn anger into hatred. When anger lasts more than an hour is really potential hatred. Once hatred sets in, a difficult person is born within you; and you may soon find humiliating another person becomes a normal, or even delightful, activity.

Nurture a sense of humor.

This is very important. It will keep your sanity intact amid the fiercest pressure attacks. Humor keeps your LOT very high, not to mention a healthy heart and lasting youth. It keeps everything light and easy, even in the worst scenario. Always find something funny in whatever is happening. As the adage goes, laughter is the best medicine. A sense of humor can change persons and tight situations.

Watch your health and diet.

It's hard to control your anger when you're sick, especially with hypertension or heart ailments. So eat healthy foods, especially those high in fiber. Avoid fatty and salty foods, unhealthy drinks, junk foods, and those high in cholesterol. Take natural food supplements high in micro-nutrients, and exercise regularly. Try to maintain your ideal weight. Get enough sleep to get ready for tomorrow's new pressures Your LOT can cope better with pressures if your health doesn't get in the way.

CHAPTER 9- HOW TO AVOID CONFRONTATIONS WITH DIFFICULT PEOPLE

Some situations with difficult people tend to tighten too much. At times you have to get out of them for a while to breathe in fresh strength again, and later go back to the same situation to conquer it. This kind of getting out is temporary, and is not meant to avoid difficult people altogether.

Joining to Conquer a Difficult Person/Situation

You can join forces with your siblings to appease your difficult parents, or you may unite with other workers in pacifying a difficult boss. There's safety and strength in numbers. You can encourage each other whenever the pressure gets too strong. You can help each other out in getting jobs done right.

Children can agree to lessen added hassles by avoiding friction between themselves (They can appear to be more acceptable to their difficult parents). If a solo performance of good attitude can do wonders to change difficult people, then just imagine what a positive group of people can do? A proverb says that two heads are better than one. It's not an alien from another planet that's being portrayed here, but a unity in working out a positive course of action. Joint acts of goodness are sure to overwhelm a single difficult person.

Reverse Psychology Works Wonders

Most difficult people, being egoistic, are childish. Most tricks for spoiled kids are applicable to them. It pays to study how to pacify tots in tantrums and apply that to difficult adults.

Reverse psychology is basically suggesting the positive opposite. It requires a touch of art to skillfully apply this. Let's say a difficult person interferes while you're giving an inspiring talk to a small group. He hints out that he knows better than you do. So you stop and let the guy have his say. Limit his time, then say something like: "That was interesting. After I finish, I'm sure some of you here also want to say something." Stress the words "After I finish." This will give a hint to all, especially to Mr. Difficult Guy, that you don't want any interruption until you are done talking.

The famous sermon on the mount, given by Jesus, taught that it pays to always do more than is being asked by difficult people. If they ask you to carry a bag in one mile, carry it two miles. If they ask for your cloak, give them your other garments as well. If they slap you on the right cheek, offer the other as well. In this way, the sermon tells us you "heap up burning coals in their heads." This means you make them re-think their behavior compared to yours. The re-thinking can only happen if those difficult people see something different and positive in you. If you confront them head-on, then you have just proven yourself to be another difficult person.

Laugh Them Off

Long time ago, colonized people used comedy plays to protest the cruelty of their colonizers in a light way. They communicated the message to both countrymen and oppressors effectively by making fun of everyday scenes of injustices.

Humor can drive the point home without directly condemning the offenders. It can make both the offending and offended parties laugh and yet learn. In one Christmas party I attended, the employees thought of presenting a comedy skit where both employees and employers were impersonated in a comical way. They all saw themselves in a new light. They realized their strengths and weaknesses, as well as what images they have been projecting to others. If difficult people try to make everyone see how ugly you are, you may start calling them Mr. Handsome or Miss Beautiful, not with a look of insult but with sincerity. Mean it. It will either make them feel ashamed of themselves, so they will stop; or they will feel accomplished, so they will mellow down because they think they have proven their point.

Go to Your Happy Place When Difficult People Bully You

When under attack, relax. You can't die of severe attacks from difficult people unless you choose to. If you think too highly of yourself (that's feeding the ego), chances are you will easily be offended by difficult people. On the other hand, if you estimate yourself just right, and you don't pay attention to what difficult people think about you (because you know better than to take their remarks seriously), no damage will be done no matter how severe the attacks. You can just smile away at the offenders.

Relaxing is one of the greater virtues not even the most extremely wealthy people possess. For sure, difficult people can never relax because they don't know how. They actually hate the idea. Relaxation to them is mortal sin. Thus, they also deprive people around them of rest and relaxation. They need to see that everybody is pressured. But once they see that you can relax under attack, they will begin to avoid you. They may spread the news around that you are lazy and won't amount to anything. To them, tension leads to sure success. Not only can you save yourself from difficult people by relaxing, you can also maintain good health.

Practice relaxing in any situation: While reading, eating, conversing, sitting or standing, walking, catching a bus, being scolded, in an emergency, etc. It will be difficult at first; but as you practice, it will become spontaneous. The body can be taught and conditioned by the mind. Don't surrender your fate to circumstances around you.

Never control others (that's being a difficult person), but learn to control yourself. Many say it is important to let your temper show, because repressed emotions are bad for the heart. Relaxing is not repressing anything in you. Uncontrolled tempers only make matters worse. There is a saying that a fool gives full bent to his emotions, but the wise refrains from them. So at the first sign of a threat from difficult people, relax. Don't let their wishes dictate how you live your life.

Speak Up

There will be times when difficult people become too intolerable, especially when other people are greatly affected. During these rare times, you must speak out and rebuke the offenders gently. There was once a difficult young man who was giving an old lady a hard time on a train. A young lady stood up and asked him to be patient with the old woman then invited him to join her in giving the old woman a hand. When I was in a conference once, a difficult person stood up to ask lots of questions that led nowhere. The speaker gently cut him short and then said, "I will answer one question, sir, but the rest of your questions will be dealt with after my speech so we will not run out of time."

Sometimes, difficult people must be shown that they have gone beyond their limits. But this must be done gently and free from any harmful intention, especially from public humiliation. We don't want to merely stop difficult people; we also want to help them.

Focus on Other Positives

When difficult people start hammering away at you, try to divert your attention to positive things. If a difficult spouse is consistently nagging about your son's failing grades in math or science, shift your spouse's attention to subjects where your son got better grades. Learn to take attention away from an unwanted subject matter.

Another technique of shifting attention is to pass the pressure on to others. This is very effective in a public speaking situation. You may find this handy in a small group discussion where you act as a speaker or lecturer. If a difficult person is asking you senseless (those that have no connection whatsoever to the topic) questions, or if that individual just wants to interfere with the discussion, you may either: 1. Entertain questions later (which is a temporary diversionary technique); or 2. Deal with the question now by throwing the same question to the group.

Putting It In Black and White

When dealing with difficult people, especially in sensitive matters like favors, money, or appointments, it will help you to put everything in writing. Companies make policies precisely for dealing with difficult employees. When difficult friends or relatives borrow a big sum of money from you, have them sign an agreement to pay the price on a definite date. This is ideal for those who have a track record of unpaid debts. If an appointment for a meeting is set with difficult people, keep repeating to them the details. If possible, let them text to your cell phone the time and place so you may have a record of your appointment that they themselves have set up.

If difficult employees insist on something unreasonable, it is safe to make policies or regulations regarding employee rights, duties, and privileges which employees have to sign as part of their work contract. You can go back to the provisions of these policies or regulations as you deal with them in the future. Difficult people are so finicky about whatever details they can use to annoy people and to prove to them that they have erred. Difficult people enjoy it when they catch a person unprepared and at a loss. Thus, you may have to deal with them according to their ways. A proverb says: "At times we must deal with fools according to their foolishness; though at times, we must also deal with them differently."

Going Against the Flow

There are times you must remain meek and silent as you deal with difficult people. There are times you must go with their line of thinking for a while to ease their pressures. But there are times you have to shut them up without losing your dignity. But then there are times you have to simply do the opposite of what they want you to do. If they make fun of you, you simply look at them and ask, "So I look stupid. What's so funny about that?" In doing this, make sure there are no other people around, or these difficult people may get what they want, and everybody may end up laughing at you. If this happens, laugh with them. This will neutralize the situation. At times you have to shut your mouth if these difficult people goad you to speak. Or speak when they want you to shut your mouth. But do this without any ill feelings against the offenders. Just teach them a lesson. It must be stressed that this strategy is not always advisable. You must be keenly sensitive to situations before you can masterfully apply this technique.

Applicability of techniques is on a case-to-case basis. Hence, dealing with difficult people takes lots of practice to master. Don't be afraid to commit mistakes. Mistakes, when taken with maturity, will make us wiser. The wiser we get, the more we master, and the more we can help.

Leaving the "Show"

When things really get out of hand and every option has become useless, the best thing to do to be free from a tight situation is to excuse yourself from the scene politely. Just leave. There's no use spending your energy in fighting a dragon like Don Quixote. But make sure you excuse yourself gracefully so as not to lose face. Smile. Chin up. Make sure your last note is a friendly one. Of course, difficult people will think that they have won that round. But that's the way they always think. You can never make them think otherwise. So why fuss? Let them think all they want. What matters most is that you attain peace and solitude.

Chapter 10- Bonus: Learn the Powerful Secret in Dealing with a Difficult Person

Do you want to know a powerful secret that everyone should know but few people do? Whether we know it or not, the most precious possession for every human being is his ego. This does not mean that the person is "egotistical" in the pejorative sense of the word. What we are talking about is a sense of human dignity that we are all born with. It's a knowledge deep in each man or woman's heart that he or she is important and deserves respect. This is the true basis for self-esteem. It's a healthy force and a birthright. People who don't understand this often try to become significant through making money, becoming famous, or gaining power or significance in many different ways. This can cause a person to become an egotist in the negative sense, but that never satisfies the hunger for true inner self-esteem since it doesn't get to the root of real self-esteem. This unsatisfied yearning for self-esteem creates most of the trouble in the world and also in the psyches of difficult people. If we remember a few truths about ourselves and everyone else, it will help us have much more successful relationships and encounters with others.

Remember, 1. We all care more about ourselves than anything else in the world. There's nothing wrong with this. It's how we survive. 2. Every person wants to feel significant. 3. Every person craves approval by others, so that he can approve of himself. We need to have some self-esteem before we can be kind to others. We need to like ourselves, at least to some extent, before we can like others. Knowing this helps us to understand why others act badly sometimes, and possibly why we do, too.

When self-esteem is good, people are easy to get along with. Their positive qualities dominate. They are tolerant and willing to listen to others' points-of-view. They can admit to being wrong sometimes since this is not crushing to their healthy self-esteem. When self-esteem is low, people are difficult to get along with. People who come on as bullies or blowhards do so because of low self-esteem, not high self-esteem. When self-esteem is low, even a critical glance or slightly negative remark can have a severe sting.

Can you see the lesson here? The way to deal with this difficult person (all difficult people) is to help him like himself better. And do it in a genuine, authentic way, not in a superior, patronizing way. We all have good qualities as well as bad. Can you find the good qualities in the difficult person? If so, you will be able to treat him with respect. He will recognize that you have respect for him and will be easier to communicate with, now and in the future.

What Makes Difficult People Difficult?
Remember, we all have a deep hunger for respect, and if you treat others with respect, they will be much easier to get along with.

About the Author

Ronald Smith is a known resource speaker, who has graced several conventions and seminars throughout Asia and the US. When not public speaking and writing, Ronald enjoys long walks down the beach with his wife, Emily.